La Jolla Playhouse

YMCA

Gilman Dr

La Jolla Scenic Dr N

Torrey Pines Rd

La Jolla Village Dr

52

5

5

Soledad Mountain Rd

Kate Sessions Park

Soledad Rd

LA JOLLA ALTA

Cardeno Dr

Foothill Blvd

Fanuel St

La Jolla Pkwy

Mt Soledad National Veterans Memorial

All Hallows

Via Capri

La Jolla Scenic Dr S

La Jolla Mesa Dr

Mushroom House

Birch Aquarium

Scripps Institution of Oceanography

La Jolla Shores Dr

LA JOLLA SHORES

La Jolla Beach & Tennis Club

Scripps Pier

La Jolla Shores Beach

MUIRLANDS WEST

MUIRLANDS

Nautilus St

Turquoise St

La Jolla Blvd

BIRD ROCK

San Diego-La Jolla Underwater Park

Torrey Pines Rd

La Jolla Country Club

Coggan Family Aquatic Complex

La Jolla High School

La Jolla United Methodist

Coast Walk

The Cave Store

La Jolla Cove

Point La Jolla
Scripps Park
Boomer Beach

Shell Beach

Wall St

Girard Ave

Fay Ave

VILLAGE OF LA JOLLA

Prospect St

La Jolla Rec Center

La Jolla Blvd

Children's Pool

Museum of Contemporary Art San Diego

The Bishop's School

Coast Blvd Park

Wipeout Beach

Whispering Sands Beach

Marine St Beach

Windansea Beach

La Jolla

JEWEL BY THE SEA

December 25, 2018
Merry Christmas,
Kevin !
Love, mom

La Jolla

JEWEL BY THE SEA

Ann Collins

SUNBELT PUBLICATIONS, INC.
San Diego, California

La Jolla: Jewel by the Sea

Sunbelt Publications, Inc.
Copyright © 2018 by Ann Collins
All rights reserved. First edition 2018

Book and cover design by Ann Collins
Project management by Deborah Young
Printed in China by Four Colour Print Group, Louisville, Kentucky

No part of this book may be reproduced in any form without permission
from the publisher. Please direct comments and inquiries to:
Sunbelt Publications, Inc.
P.O. Box 191126
San Diego, CA 92159-1126
(619) 258-4911, fax: (619) 258-4916
www.sunbeltpublications.com

21 20 19 18   4 3 2 1

Library of Congress Cataloging-in-Publication Data

Names: Collins, Ann Marie.
Title: La Jolla : jewel by the sea / by Ann Collins.
Other titles: La Jolla, jewel by the sea
Description: First edition. | San Diego, California : Sunbelt Publications, Inc., [2018]
Identifiers: LCCN 2018026474 | ISBN 9781941384435 (hardcover : alk. paper)
Subjects: LCSH: La Jolla (San Diego, Calif.)--Pictorial works. | La Jolla
  (San Diego, Calif.)--Description and travel. | La Jolla (San Diego, Calif.)--Biography.
Classification: LCC F869.S22 L35 2018 | DDC 979.4/98500222--dc23
  LC record available at https://lccn.loc.gov/2018026474

All photographs by Ann Collins, except where noted below:

Endpapers: Maps by Kathy Wise and map illustrations by
    Lori Mitchell.

Page 1: Alice Douglas at age three photo courtesy of the
    Dolan/Collins family archives.

Page 16: Ellen Browning Scripps photo from the Collection
    of the La Jolla Historical Society.

Page 35: Cliff Robertson photo from the Collection of the
    La Jolla Historical Society.

Page 39: Gene Littler photo by Lester Nehamkin from the
    Collection of the La Jolla Historical Society.

Page 55: Carl Ekstrom photo, © Robert Wald, *The Ocean
    Magazine.*

Page 59: Raquel Welch photo from the San Diego History
    Center.

Page 60: Gregory Peck photo from the Collection of the
    La Jolla Historical Society.

Page 72: William J. "Bill" Kellogg photo courtesy of the
    La Jolla Beach & Tennis Club.

Page 77: Dr. Roger Revelle photo from the San Diego
    History Center.

Page 81: Theodor and Audrey Geisel photo from the
    Collection of the La Jolla Historical Society, courtesy
    of Carol Sonstein Photography.

Page 82: Dr. Irwin M. Jacobs photo courtesy of Qualcomm
    Incorporated.

Whispering Sands Beach.

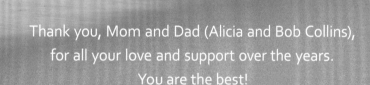

Thank you, Mom and Dad (Alicia and Bob Collins),
for all your love and support over the years.
You are the best!

Acknowledgments

Many people have helped me in the creation of *La Jolla: Jewel by the Sea*. I am grateful to Mary Lee Delafield for suggesting that I make a coffee table photo book of La Jolla. Thanks go to Susan Rosenberg for her editing skills and to Beth Wagner Brust for loaning me her collection of books about our hometown and for reading my first draft.

The La Jolla Historical Society and its dedicated staff through the years deserve many accolades for their efforts to preserve La Jolla's history. The information in their publications and archives and the books written by local historians have been invaluable to the creation of this book.

To all the people who provided me with information and the photos of notable La Jollans, thank you. I also want to thank Kathy Wise for her graphic design insights, Lori Mitchell for her cute map illustrations, and the folks at Sunbelt Publications for taking a chance on my book.

Introduction

Boogie boarding at La Jolla Shores when the ocean warms in the summer. Chasing sea gulls away from chip bags left on beach towels. Snorkeling with the leopard sharks. Hearing the echoing wash of water inside Sunny Jim Cave. Sitting in my beach chair with a good book at Coast Boulevard Park. Scanning the horizon for whale spouts. Listening to the barks of the harbor seals and sea lions. Driving past the Windansea shack to check out the surf. Riding my bike up to the Mount Soledad Cross (though *not* from the steep Via Capri side). Watching the paragliders soar along the cliffs at Torrey Pines. Running into family and friends while doing errands or strolling around "the village," as downtown La Jolla has been known since its early days. Grabbing a sandwich at Girard Gourmet. Roaming the book section of Warwick's. And photographing sunsets from anywhere along La Jolla's coastline. These are the things that mean "home" to me.

I was born in the village when Scripps Memorial Hospital was located on Prospect Street. When I was a child, I started taking photos with Instamatic film cameras. At La Jolla High School I wrote articles while on the newspaper staff. As I have grown so has La Jolla, but the community's small-town atmosphere remains, and the ocean, coastline, and climate can't be beat. La Jolla is a jewel by the sea.

The origin of the name "La Jolla" has never been definitively determined, but the most popular theory is that it came from the Spanish words "la joya" (the jewel), which are pronounced the same. Spain colonized California in earnest during the 1700s when the missions were established. Spanish influence is visible all over La Jolla from street names to architecture.

La Jolla's development began in 1887. Despite its individual character, it is not its own town. It is an upscale, seaside community that lies within the city limits of San Diego, California.

A sea lion warms itself in the late-afternoon sun at Point La Jolla.

A tremendous number of people have positively impacted La Jolla since its beginning. Ellen Browning Scripps takes top honors. La Jolla would not be what it is today without her foresight, generosity, caring attitude, and love of home. In the pages of this book, I have featured Miss Scripps and a number of other notable La Jollans who have given of their time and money; have served on civic and/or cultural committees; or have achieved success through inventions, business, talent, skill, intellect, creativity, or all of the above. They are inspirational members of the community.

I hope you enjoy reading about these fascinating people and the La Jolla history accompanying the photos of my hometown.

Ann Collins
Photographer/Writer

Point La Jolla.

La Jolla Cove

La Jolla Cove has been a popular destination for generations. Horse-drawn buggies and wagons brought visitors here beginning in the late 1800s. Today, families, open water swimmers, snorkelers, scuba divers, and kayakers enjoy the San Diego-La Jolla Underwater Park and Ecological Reserve, which encompasses the Cove. The reserve is a look-but-don't-touch-or-take area that protects the marine life. Since 1916 open water swimmers have competed here. The La Jolla Rough Water Swim has attracted as many as 2,000 competitors aged 5 to 85; however, the increasing numbers of harbor seals and sea lions have led organizers to cancel the event due to the potential for poor water quality.

The author/photographer's family had early ties to San Diego. Her maternal grandmother, Alice Douglas Dolan, played at the Cove as a child. Here in 1903, at age three, Alice and her aunt Mary are seated beside the glass bottom boats that allowed visitors to witness the wonders of the undersea world before the existence of masks and snorkels.

Seven Sisters Caves

Along the cliffs above the Seven Sisters Caves, cormorants roost in the trees and on the exposed cliff faces. Brown pelicans and gulls perch on the bluffs. Sea lions and harbor seals sun themselves on rocks and swim among the kayakers and snorkelers.

The Cave Store

Seven Sisters Caves indent the cliffs along the coast near La Jolla Cove. The Sunny Jim Sea Cave is the largest and only one accessible by land—from inside The Cave Store on Coast Boulevard. In 1902 German Gustav Schultz, a civil engineer and professor of geology, purchased the land. The hand-hewn tunnel was dug out with picks and shovels. Before the stairs were built, visitors had to hold onto a rope to go down and back up. L. Frank Baum, author of *The Wonderful Wizard of Oz*, named the cave for its silhouette resembling the Sunny Jim character created for a wheat flakes cereal advertising campaign. Today 145 steps slope to the sea, where the water level rises and falls with the tides and surf, and the sound seems to echo inside the cave.

Coast Walk

It's possible that Native Americans—the Kumeyaay—once walked the path now known as the La Jolla Coast Walk Trail. It begins at Goldfish Point near The Cave Store and meanders along the cliff tops, above the Seven Sisters Caves, then out to Torrey Pines Road.

Brockton Villa

Designated as a San Diego Historical Landmark, Brockton Villa Restaurant provides coastal dining in an 1894 beach bungalow above La Jolla Cove. The bungalow was originally built as a weekend retreat. One of its second owners, real estate agent Nellie Mills, named it for her relationship to Brockton, Massachusetts. Bob Sinclair, founder of Pannikin Coffee and Tea, leased the property in the early 1990s. Committed to the preservation of La Jolla's architectural heritage, Sinclair renovated the aged structure and opened it as a restaurant.

Congregational Church of La Jolla

In 1889 La Jolla was a tiny community. Episcopalians, Presbyterians, and Congregationalists worshiped together in fellowship. Today they all have their own churches. The current Congregational Church of La Jolla has been on Cave Street since 1916. During the centennial in 2016, a time capsule in a mason jar was excavated from the building's cornerstone. Like uncovering buried treasure, church members found coins, photos, letters, newspaper articles, and church programs from the early 1900s.

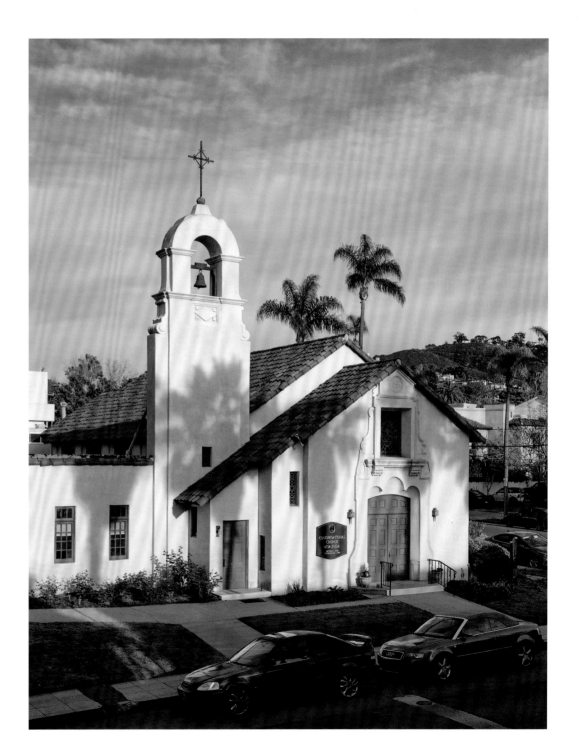

Children's Pool

Ellen Browning Scripps wanted to protect the beach-going children of San Diego from dangerous ocean currents and waves. The 300-foot breakwater wall she funded took at least ten years to complete, opening in the early 1930s. The Children's Pool beach has also been called the Casa Beach or Casa Pool for its proximity to Casa de Mañana, a former hotel that became an upscale retirement community. During winter storms, sometimes the breakwater isn't even enough to protect beachgoers. This January 1988 storm created rough seas and a dramatic display of Mother Nature's power.

Since 1979 the growing population of Pacific harbor seals has been steadily taking over the Children's Pool, creating controversy over its intended use. The harbor seals haul out on beaches and rocks to rest and warm up. From December through May, the females give birth and raise their pups here, necessitating the beach's closure to people.

14

Ellen Browning Scripps

Miss Ellen Browning Scripps liked to make a difference without anyone feeling indebted to her. "But I do like to see and know any benefits that accrue from my giving," she said. Miss Scripps was born in 1836 in London, England, and immigrated to the United States at age seven with her widowed father and five siblings. They settled in Illinois where Mr. Scripps remarried and fathered more children. Ellen's love of learning and the wages she earned from a teaching position allowed her to enroll at Knox College in an era when few women attended college. Afterwards, she worked again as a teacher, then as a copy editor and writer for a newspaper owned by one of her brothers. A second brother also started a Midwestern newspaper business. Ellen invested her savings in both. Her investments did well over the years, and she also inherited money, which she wanted to put to good use, especially in her adopted community of La Jolla. She fell in love with La Jolla during a visit and in 1897 built a home here. She called it South Moulton Villa. In an 1899 speech she said, "It lies with us residents and owners of La Jolla to make 'our jewel' what we will, only keeping it always in harmony with its glorious natural setting." Miss Scripps was a patron of the arts, of science, education, preservation, and recreation. Her generosity has touched generations of lives.

Museum of Contemporary Art San Diego

Ellen Browning Scripps built her first home—South Moulton Villa—on Prospect Street in 1897. When it burned as a result of arson in 1915, the elderly Miss Scripps hired architect Irving J. Gill to build what she hoped would be a fireproof residence that could, after her death, be used in some practical way by the community. Its central location in the village made it an ideal place for something special. Her wish was realized when The Art Center of La Jolla opened here in the early 1940s, later becoming the La Jolla Museum of Art, La Jolla Museum of Contemporary Art, and then Museum of Contemporary Art San Diego. It is dedicated to artworks created since 1950. A substantial renovation will make more room for the growing collection.

Wisteria Cottage

Every spring purple wisteria blossoms cascade over the pergola entrance to the La Jolla Historical Society's Wisteria Cottage. The bungalow was built in 1904 and is a San Diego Historical Landmark. Miss Eliza "Virginia" Scripps called it home and named it for the wisteria. Cobblestones embedded in the walls, columns, and foundation came from the shoreline in Bird Rock. In 1942 Wisteria Cottage became home to the Balmer School for children, the beginnings of what is now known as La Jolla Country Day School. John Cole's Book Shop resided in the cottage for many years, filling the cozy rooms with books about travel, the arts, and more. Today Wisteria Cottage hosts changing exhibitions related to La Jolla and San Diego history.

Wipeout Beach

Along Coast Boulevard, below the Museum of Contemporary Art San Diego, lies Wipeout Beach. The south end is favored by skimboarders, but strong currents can make swimming here dangerous.

St. James by-the-Sea

In early La Jolla a small congregation of Episcopalians regularly met in Eliza "Virginia" Scripps's Wisteria Cottage on Prospect Street. Virginia's half-sister, Ellen, donated the property across from the cottage to what became St. James by-the-Sea Episcopal Church. The original building was constructed in the Spanish Colonial style. By 1929 a larger church was needed to accommodate the growing congregation. The first building was moved, and a second one was opened in 1930. Ellen Browning Scripps had gifted the bell tower to the church a few years earlier in memory of Virginia who had died in 1921.

Grande Colonial

The Grande Colonial on Prospect Street has been welcoming guests since 1913 when it opened its doors as the Colonial Apartments and Hotel. Renovations over the years have updated the historic hotel while maintaining its original elegance and dignified grandeur. Its award-winning restaurant, Nine-Ten, was once the location of the La Jolla Drug Store, which featured a popular ice cream parlor. The pharmacist was the father of future movie star Gregory Peck. When Peck and others founded the La Jolla Playhouse in 1947, many of the performers stayed at the Colonial. These included David Niven, Jane Wyatt, Groucho Marx, Eve Arden, and Charlton Heston. Some of the hotel's early guests may still be on the premises as there are rumors of several interesting and fun-loving ghosts.

Shell Beach

Hunting for shells is best done at Shell Beach during low tide. Access to
the beach is from the south end of Ellen Browning Scripps Park.

The Bishop's School

Ellen Browning Scripps, a former teacher, believed that schools should be "an open door to knowledge." She was one of the founders of The Bishop's School, which admitted students in 1909 in the heart of La Jolla. Part of the school's mission is the pursuit of "intellectual, artistic and athletic excellence in the context of the Episcopal tradition." Originally a private boarding school for girls preparing to attend "the best Eastern colleges," Bishop's is now a coed independent day school for grades six through twelve. The students come from all over San Diego County. Ellen Scripps and her half-sister Virginia gave land and financial support to the school and hired renowned architect Irving J. Gill to begin what has become a beautiful campus of historic and contemporary buildings.

St. Mary's Chapel and the Bishop Johnson Memorial Tower were designed by Carleton Monroe Winslow in 1917 and 1930, respectively. Right Reverend Joseph Horsfall Johnson, first Bishop of the Episcopal Diocese of Los Angeles, was one of the school's founders.

La Jolla Recreation Center

The La Jolla Community House and Playground opened to the public in 1915, a gift from Ellen Browning Scripps to the children and residents of La Jolla. Public playgrounds were uncommon back then, and this playground became a model for others in the United States. Miss Scripps hired architect Irving J. Gill to design a building that would contain meeting rooms and a performance hall. The name eventually changed to the La Jolla Recreation Center. The Rec Center still serves as a meeting place for La Jolla's civic groups.

La Jolla Presbyterian

Growth and expansion have characterized the La Jolla Presbyterian Church since 1905 when members of the congregation met in a wood-floored tent. Their pastor traveled between preaching services in La Jolla and Pacific Beach. The First Presbyterian Church of La Jolla, as it was known then, quickly took up residence in their three-room "Little Brown Church" at Girard Avenue and Torrey Pines Road. However, that location was considered a bit far out of town. The church building was hauled two blocks closer into the heart of the village. As the church's growth continued, land was acquired on Draper Avenue and buildings were constructed. It wasn't always easy, but as their historian wrote in a 1955 golden anniversary publication, "Christian charity, faith and trust combine with courage and industry to pioneer and build."

Boomer Beach

South of Point La Jolla, near La Jolla Cove, Boomer Beach receives sizable waves. Experienced body surfers favor the break here, but submerged rocks add to the danger.

Athenaeum Music & Arts Library

The Reading Room of the Library Association of La Jolla welcomed patrons in 1899 at the corner of Wall Street and Girard Avenue. As the population of La Jolla grew so did the library. A new building was designed in the Spanish Colonial Revival style. The Athenaeum portion was added later to house the association's collection of art and music books. The ongoing need for more room ultimately sent what had become La Jolla's public library to a new building on Draper Avenue. The Athenaeum Music & Arts Library stayed and expanded into the vacated quarters on Wall Street, creating a gallery space and reading room. The Athenaeum offers art exhibits, classes, concerts, special events, lectures, and workshops.

La Jolla Post Office

During the Great Depression, President Franklin D. Roosevelt's New Deal created the Works Progress Administration (WPA) to employ people in need of work and to stimulate the U.S. economy. The construction of La Jolla's post office on Wall Street was part of this work program. Before then the post office had been housed in private homes or storefronts. Completed in 1935, the Spanish Colonial Revival-style building is on the National Register of Historic Places.

LA JOLLA POST OFFICE, 1935

COMMEMORATING THE 75TH ANNIVERSARY OF
THE LA JOLLA POST OFFICE BUILDING
AND LOBBY MURAL BY ARTIST
BELLE BARANCEANU

UNDER THE WORKS PROGRESS ADMINISTRATION

LA JOLLA HISTORICAL SOCIETY, SEPTEMBER 2010

Belle Baranceanu Mural

The lobby of the La Jolla Post Office features a colorful mural by renowned early twentieth-century artist Belle Baranceanu. Her art depicts a view of La Jolla's northern coast from high above the village on Hillside Drive.

Marine Street Beach

Homes now occupy what were once barren sand dunes along this beach.
Village residents back in the early 1900s considered this area to the south
remote and isolated, but a number of hardy souls developed it. Street
names such as Marine Street and Sea Lane identify neighboring beaches.
Whispering Sands lies to the north. Horseshoe Reef is the surf break offshore.

Cliff Robertson

Aviator, writer, humanitarian, World War II veteran, and Academy Award-winning actor Cliff Robertson caught lobsters from his skiff off Windansea Beach as a boy. In 1925 he was born in La Jolla and raised by relatives, primarily his grandmother. His passion for flying began at age five when he witnessed a plane doing acrobatic moves over La Jolla. He also loved the beach, especially Marine Street Beach on the edge of the Barber Tract neighborhood. Developer Philip Barber built Robertson's small skiff. Many years later Robertson renewed his ties to La Jolla when he bought Barber's former home, Casa de la Paz, overlooking Marine Street Beach. After carefully renovating it, he had it designated as a historic landmark to protect it. In his own words, "I could not and never would abandon my hometown La Jolla."

Girard Gourmet

Since 1987 Girard Gourmet has been preparing and serving made-to-order deli sandwiches, organic salads, hot entrées, baked goods, and decorative cookies. Owners François and Diana Goedhuys even have their own farm near Julian to provide fresh produce for their popular restaurant and catering business. Lucky schoolchildren at the San Diego French-American School in La Jolla get to enjoy lunches prepared by Girard Gourmet.

Warwick's

The arts and culture have always been important to La Jollans. This includes books.
Redding's Book Store in La Jolla was founded in 1902. It became Warwick's in
1939. William T. Warwick, a widower and career bookseller who had opened his
first Warwick's in Minnesota in 1896, relocated to La Jolla, where his sister lived.
He purchased Redding's and later married the widowed Mrs. Redding. In addition
to being a bookstore, Warwick's is known for its selection of fine stationery, unusual
gifts, and office and art supplies. Author events and book signings regularly bring in
customers. According to fourth-generation owner Nancy Warwick, the store "is the
oldest continuously family-owned and operated bookstore in the United States."

La Jolla Country Club

Active La Jollans began playing golf as early as 1899 when the roads were dirt and few homes had been built. Located above and behind the village, the La Jolla Country Club got its start in 1913 with a nine-hole golf course. Seven years later grass replaced "greens" made of oil and sand. The course later expanded to 18 holes, and prominent golf tournaments were played here. Members moved into a permanent clubhouse in 1927 and have enjoyed spectacular views of La Jolla and the coastline ever since.

Gene Littler

When his mother made a hole-in-one at the La Jolla Country Club in January 1942, eleven-year-old Gene Littler understood the significance. He had practically grown up on the club's course and was already a strong player himself. In 1953 he won a professional tournament as an amateur. After going pro, Littler won the 1961 U.S. Open and 28 other PGA Tour events. Seven Ryder Cup teams benefitted from his participation. Many golfers envied Littler his consistent and rhythmic swing, which earned him the moniker "Gene the Machine." His 25th tour victory held the most meaning for him. It came after he was diagnosed and treated for cancer. In 1990 Littler was inducted into the World Golf Hall of Fame.

Harry's Coffee Shop

Harry Rudolph, Jr., loved baseball and his hometown team, the Brooklyn Dodgers. He even worked as a batboy for them. When the team moved from New York to Los Angeles, Harry followed, ending up in La Jolla. In 1960 he, his wife, and his parents opened Harry's Coffee Shop on Girard Avenue. The classic American diner became a popular meeting place and a community-oriented family business that has sponsored many youth sports teams over the years. It is still family owned and serves up a friendly welcome and breakfast all day.

Mary, Star of the Sea

In 1906 La Jolla's first Catholic parish—Mary, Star of the Sea, dedicated to the Blessed Virgin Mary—was established in the village. The current church building was designed in 1936 in the Contemporary Spanish Mission style. A fresco painted by Alfredo Ramos Martinez rises above the entrance to greet parishioners.

Adelaide's Flowers

In 1936 Adelaide's Flowers began as a flower stand along Highway 101 in Encinitas, California. Adelaide Phillips founded what would become a multi-generational business dedicated to beautiful floral designs and caring customer service. She moved her shop to La Jolla around the early 1950s. Though no longer owned by the family today, Adelaide's tradition of creativity, quality, and attention to detail continues.

Farmers Market

On Sundays throughout the year, vendors at the La Jolla Open Aire Market sell fresh produce, crafts, art, and tasty treats on the grounds of La Jolla Elementary School. The food court offers a choice of international dishes and a covered eating area. Proceeds from the farmers market benefit the school.

Coast Boulevard Park

The grass-covered bluff of Coast Boulevard Park attracts sunset viewers and picnickers. Wedding parties enjoy the coastal beauty from the north end in the somewhat concealed Cuvier Park, also called the "Wedding Bowl." The rocky shoreline is a favorite tide-pooling spot at low tide. Artistic rock formations attract photographers at sunset. Hospital Point, aka Hospitals, was named by surfers for the original Scripps Memorial Hospital on Prospect Street and medical buildings on Coast Boulevard that could be seen from the water like a navigational aid.

Concours d'Elegance

Each spring, the La Jolla Historical Society presents the La Jolla Concours d'Elegance & Motor Car Classic. Ellen Browning Scripps Park becomes a seaside outdoor museum for automobile enthusiasts. Classic cars in pristine condition are on display and compete for honors and bragging rights. The fundraiser is open to the public and benefits several local organizations.

La Valencia Hotel

The La Valencia Hotel, also known as the "Pink Lady" and "La V," opened its doors in December 1926 and has been lovingly preserved ever since. Designed in the Spanish Colonial Revival style, she is listed as a member of the Historic Hotels of America: National Trust for Historic Preservation. During World War II, the tower was used as a lookout post manned by local residents and sometimes even hotel guests. They searched the sea for enemy vessels and the sky for enemy aircraft. In 1956 the historic Cabrillo Hotel next door was integrated into the La Valencia. Hollywood stars such as Tony Curtis, Lucille Ball, Dustin Hoffman, Sophia Loren, and many others have stayed at the La V.

At the La Valencia, the perfect Mediterranean palette of colors is created by the hotel's pool, Ellen Browning Scripps Park, the Pacific coast around La Jolla Cove, and brilliant bougainvillea.

Half Marathon

When spring comes, the Kiwanis Club of La Jolla hosts the scenic and fun La Jolla Half Marathon & Shores 5K. Some runners wear costumes. Others race with groups of friends. Competitors reach the finish line at Ellen Browning Scripps Park with wide smiles and a huge sense of accomplishment. The sponsored event attracts more than 6,000 participants, whose entry fees benefit children in San Diego and La Jolla.

Meanley's Hardware

Meanley & Son Hardware opened for business in 1948 on Girard Avenue. Their popcorn machine enticed customers into the store for many of those years. The Meanley family, related to philanthropist Ellen Browning Scripps, founded the store as a way to be of service to the La Jolla community. In 1997 Meanley's partnered with the Ace Hardware Co-op. The store continues its mission of service to others by supporting children's causes and providing customers with cookware, garden tools, paint, hardware, and gadgets of all kinds.

51

YMCA

La Jolla's renovated, improved, and expanded YMCA on Cliffridge Avenue feels like active resort living with an ocean view. A $5 million donation from the Dan McKinney family—La Jolla residents since the 1950s—jumpstarted the fundraising campaign for the four-phase project completed in 2018 and renamed the Dan McKinney Family YMCA. The late Mr. McKinney lived the Y's focus on social responsibility, "giving back and providing support to our neighbors." The Y's two other areas of focus are youth development and healthy living for everyone.

Windansea Beach

Located in a residential neighborhood at the foot of Nautilus Street and along Neptune Place, Windansea Beach is a popular spot for surfers, beachgoers, and sunset watchers. The surf shack, first built in 1946, has suffered a number of wipeouts due to high winds, high tides, large waves, and stormy conditions. Members of the surf community and volunteers from the nonprofit group Friends of WindanSea maintain the shack, rebuilding it when necessary. The San Diego Historical Resources Board designated the palm frond-covered shelter in 1998 as a historical landmark.

Winter at Windansea

The rocks at Windansea Beach are revealed each winter when strong, high waves carry the sand offshore. Most of the sand returns with the gentler waves of summer.

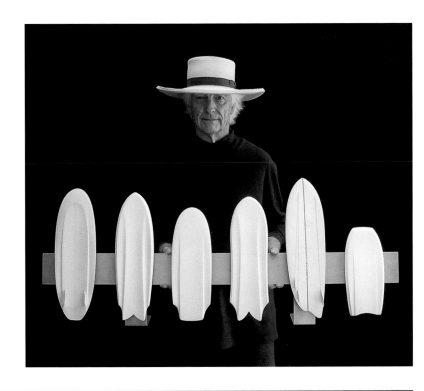

Carl Ekstrom

Carl Ekstrom has been called a "surf design guru" and a "surfboard shaper legend." A regular at Windansea in the 1950s, 1960s, and beyond, he impacted the sport with his asymmetrical surfboard design, which allows for a more maneuverable, dynamic board. He has also been involved in the development of wave machines and the boards used for riding simulated waves. He is an industrial designer who calls himself a "prototyper."

Windansea Surf Club

Founded in 1962, the Windansea Surf Club has fostered a respect for oceanic environments and produced talented surfers who have competed in worldwide surfing contests. In 1967 California Governor and future U.S. President Ronald Reagan wrote a letter of introduction and commendation on behalf of members of the Windansea Surf Club who would be traveling to and competing in Tahiti, New Caledonia, New Zealand, Australia, and Fiji. One member of the club, Mike Hynson, went on to co-star in *The Endless Summer*, a classic documentary surf film.

La Jolla United Methodist Church

The California Mission-style chapel of the
La Jolla United Methodist Church was
originally built in 1924 as the San Carlos
streetcar station. The San Diego Electric
Railway's No. 16 line ran from downtown
San Diego to the corner of Prospect Street
and Fay Avenue in La Jolla until 1940.
In a building adjacent to the station,
La Plaza restaurant and El Toro Bar
dished up Mexican food and drinks.
Legend has it that the first American
margarita drink was served at the
restaurant.

La Jolla High School

La Jolla High School first welcomed students in 1922 and is the second oldest public high school campus in the San Diego Unified School District. The school is known for its high level of academics, its theater department, and its athletics program. Home of the Vikings, its colors are red and black. Graduation takes place in June on the football field.

Coggan Family Aquatic Complex

Open to the public, the Coggan Family Aquatic Complex at La Jolla High School has been hosting swimmers and swim meets since 2002. The Olympic-size pool also serves water polo teams and matches.

Raquel Welch

Actress Raquel Welch has always been known for her beauty. She became an international sex symbol in 1966 when the film *One Million Years B.C.* was released. Her performance in *The Three Musketeers* (1973) earned her a Golden Globe Award for Best Actress. Her career in the arts began early. At La Jolla High School she was a member of the Drama Club. She was born Jo Raquel Tejada in Chicago and moved to San Diego with her family when she was two years old. Raquel kept busy in high school with clubs, student council, cheerleading, and her boyfriend, James Welch, who would later become her first husband. Outside of school she competed in beauty pageants and was crowned Miss La Jolla. In 1958 she represented the Southern California Exposition and San Diego County Fair as Fairest of the Fair. Welch was honored in 1996 with a Star on the Hollywood Walk of Fame.

La Jolla Playhouse

La Jolla residents' longtime interest in the arts took a big step forward in 1947 when the La Jolla Playhouse was established. The founding board of producers of The Actors' Company made a statement of intent that said in part, "With the La Jolla Playhouse, we hope to indicate that it is possible to combine work in motion pictures and in the theatre, and at the same time to make a contribution to the entertainment life of the community that is acting as our host." It was signed by Hollywood luminaries Mel Ferrer, Dorothy McGuire, Joseph Cotton, Jennifer Jones, and La Jolla-born Gregory Peck. The constantly changing playhouse actors traveled to La Jolla in summer and performed in the high school's auditorium. Today, the La Jolla Playhouse operates year-round in its permanent home at the University of California, San Diego. The Tony Award-winning regional theatre produces plays, musicals, and innovative performances, some of which have gone on to Broadway.

Gregory Peck

Academy Award-winning actor Gregory Peck began life in 1916 La Jolla. His father, a pharmacist, owned the La Jolla Drug Store inside the Colonial Hotel. Peck attended La Jolla Elementary School and lived with his grandmother when his parents divorced. After graduating from the University of California, Berkeley, he moved to New York to study acting and find work. He debuted on Broadway and ended up back in California performing in Hollywood films. His Oscar was awarded in 1962 for his performance in *To Kill a Mockingbird*. In 1947 he co-founded the La Jolla Playhouse. Peck also committed himself to various causes and organizations such as the American Cancer Society, the American Film Institute, and the National Council on the Arts. President Lyndon B. Johnson awarded him the Presidential Medal of Freedom.

Independence Day Fireworks

Many La Jollans enjoy celebrating the Fourth of July at Ellen Browning Scripps Park with an evening picnic, a pretty sunset, and a fireworks display. Some kayakers take in the view while floating off La Jolla Cove. The booming, colorful fireworks are not a sure thing though. A lack of sponsors and donations occasionally puts the show in jeopardy.

Scripps Park

Ellen Browning Scripps Park at La Jolla Cove began as La Jolla Park in 1887 when La Jolla was mostly barren, undeveloped land. On Miss Scripps's 91st birthday in 1927, she was informed that the park would be renamed in her honor. Scripps Park has always attracted visitors and locals as a place to have a picnic, throw a ball, stroll the coastline, watch the waves, and enjoy the sunset. Events held here include summer concerts, the Concours d'Elegance classic car show, and the finish line of the La Jolla Half Marathon.

All Hallows

La Jollans enjoy their ocean views whenever possible, even in
church. At All Hallows Catholic Church on Mount Soledad, a
wall of west-facing windows allows the congregation to take in
an inspirational view of the Pacific during Mass.

Art & Wine Festival

Lower Girard Avenue in the heart of the village becomes a pedestrian-only street for one weekend each autumn. The La Jolla Art & Wine Festival takes over with booths, a wine and beer garden, family art center, gourmet food court, roving entertainment, and live music. The annual festival is a juried art show that benefits underfunded programs at local public elementary and middle schools.

La Jolla Shores

The beach at La Jolla Shores is known for having the most gentle waves along San Diego's coastline. It was once called Long Beach because it stretches approximately one mile. Beachgoers at the Shores have plenty of activities to keep them busy: strolling, jogging, sandcastle building, kayaking, surfing, body surfing, boogie boarding, swimming, scuba diving, playing in the playground, and picnicking on the grass at Kellogg Park. In late summer leopard sharks join bathers in the warm, shallow waters at the south end. The foraging sharks are harmless to humans.

La Jolla Shores Lifeguard Station

In 2013 the new La Jolla Shores Lifeguard Station, designed by RNT Architects and consultant Hector M. Perez, won a Merit Award from the American Institute of Architects of San Diego. The tower, reminiscent of an attractive beach hut, extends up and over the boardwalk and sand. The station was designed to minimize the impact on Shores' residents' and visitors' ocean views while still allowing lifeguards to protect beachgoers.

La Jolla Beach & Tennis Club

Was there really a yacht club in La Jolla Shores? The clubhouse of the La Jolla Beach & Yacht Club held its grand opening in 1927, but the proposed harbor (today's duck pond) and channel to the ocean never worked out. When the club found itself in financial difficulty in the 1930s, F. W. Kellogg stepped in and purchased the property. Interested in tennis, he built four courts and changed the exclusive club's name to the La Jolla Beach & Tennis Club. Since 1942 the social and recreational club has hosted prestigious tournaments and attracted well-known players. It has remained in the tennis-loving Kellogg family's hands, and there are now 12 courts, as well as a nine-hole, par-three golf course; a sparkling pool; beachfront hotel rooms; and dining areas inside, poolside, and beachside.

William J. "Bill" Kellogg

The La Jolla Beach & Tennis Club has been owned and operated by four generations of Kelloggs. The family business also includes The Marine Room restaurant, La Jolla Shores Hotel, and other properties. Current president William J. "Bill" Kellogg has made his own mark on the tennis world as an avid player and competitor, as well as a supporter of tennis organizations by serving on many boards and committees. He has also been instrumental to the well-being of La Jolla, giving his time to local associations and councils. As president of the Mt. Soledad Memorial Association, he helped to save the Cross and create the National Veterans Memorial.

The Marine Room

If you dare, treat yourself to a high-tide dinner or breakfast at the historic Marine Room restaurant in La Jolla Shores. Depending on the size of the surf, waves may crash against the picture windows at your table. The restaurant first opened in 1941, but those windows didn't last. Ocean surged into the restaurant. Beginning in 1948, a span of 34 years passed without breakage. That ended in a 1982 El Niño weather year. Renovations were subsequently made, and today the award-winning Marine Room greets guests in search of seaside views, elegant cuisine, and a thrill at high tide.

Scripps Pier

Ellen Browning Scripps Memorial Pier belongs to the world-renowned Scripps Institution of Oceanography (SIO) at the north end of La Jolla Shores. The 1,090-foot-long private pier is used for research experiments, boat launching, and the collection of scientific data about La Jolla's coastal waters. Seawater needed for the laboratories and Birch Aquarium is pumped from the end of the pier, filtered, and stored in tanks. SIO's fleet of research vessels docks at the Nimitz Marine Facility on San Diego Bay. When the institution, originally the Marine Biological Association of San Diego, took up residence in the Shores in 1910, a 1,000-foot-long pier was built in 1915–16. La Jolla philanthropist Ellen Browning Scripps funded the project. In 1988 the current pier replaced the old one. It seemed only fitting that the new pier be named in honor of Miss Scripps, who was instrumental in the founding and success of SIO in its early years, along with her half-brother E. W. Scripps.

Dr. Roger Revelle

Dr. Roger Revelle guided the Scripps Institution of Oceanography (SIO) to become the internationally known and respected oceanographic institution that it is today. He received his PhD here in 1936 and served as director beginning in 1950. His wife, Ellen Virginia Clark Revelle, great-niece of philanthropist Ellen Browning Scripps, supported his work from the very beginning as well as many local causes. Dr. Revelle was a pioneer in the study of climate change and global environmental issues. President John F. Kennedy appointed him as the country's first scientific advisor to the Secretary of the Interior. From President George H. W. Bush, he received the National Medal of Science. Dr. Revelle did not content himself with just science and global issues. Locally he served as president of the La Jolla Town Council and helped bring about the creation of the University of California, San Diego (UCSD) campus, which encompasses SIO.

Birch Aquarium

The Marine Biological Association's "Little Green Laboratory" building at the La Jolla Cove housed La Jolla's first public aquarium from 1905 to 1910. When the association moved to the George H. Scripps Memorial Marine Biological Laboratory, the aquarium went with it as part of what would become Scripps Institution of Oceanography. Today the Birch Aquarium at Scripps sits on a bluff above the institution as part of the University of California, San Diego. Visitors enjoy stunning views of La Jolla Shores and the Pacific Ocean while getting their hands wet in the outdoor man-made living tide pools. Inside, the 70,000-gallon Giant Kelp Forest Tank features entertaining and educational dive shows. More than 60 habitats display the aquarium's collection of marine life and endorse its mission "to provide ocean science education, to interpret Scripps Institution of Oceanography research, and to promote ocean conservation."

Geisel Library

Architect William Perreira, known for his eye-catching, geometrical, and futuristic designs, created UCSD's Central Library. It opened in 1970 amongst the eucalyptus trees in the center of campus. In 1995 it was renamed the Geisel Library in recognition of the generous financial support from the late Theodor "Dr. Seuss" Geisel and his wife Audrey. The University of California at San Diego site had been a firing range since 1917, then a weapons training facility—Camp Matthews—during and after World War II. In 1960 the UC Regents established a San Diego campus, incorporating the Scripps Institution of Oceanography into the university.

Dr. Seuss

Colorful. Whimsical. Fun. Educational. Humorous. Wacky. Easy to read. Dr. Seuss books fit all of these descriptions. Theodor "Ted" Geisel, aka Dr. Seuss, was an imaginative writer, cartoonist, and illustrator who would sketch on whatever came to hand. While working in the publishing and advertising world of New York City, he and his first wife, Helen, visited and fell in love with La Jolla. They returned 20 years later and called it home, residing on Mount Soledad. Geisel became known and loved for his playful children's books, including *The Cat in the Hat*. After Helen died in 1967, he married Audrey Stone Dimond, whose business sense and philanthropic endeavors have kept his legacy alive. Some of his books have been adapted into plays and animated films. His list of awards includes the Pulitzer Prize and two Academy Awards. Though he died in 1991 at age 87, his books and adaptations continue to entertain people of all ages.

Snake Path

The east side of the Geisel Library features a walkable art installation called the *Snake Path* as part of the Stuart Collection. Artist Alexis Smith created the 560-foot-long path out of colored slate cut in hexagonal pieces. The "snake" slithers around a small Garden of Eden and a large granite book with a quote from John Milton's epic poem, *Paradise Lost*.

Fallen Star

A Stuart Collection art installation by Korean artist Do Ho Suh, *Fallen Star* seemingly teeters on the edge of Jacobs Hall at UCSD's Irwin & Joan Jacobs School of Engineering. The furnished Providence, Rhode Island-style house is also known as the "crooked house." It features a variety of disorienting angles that can play havoc with the senses of anyone prone to motion sickness. The artist was exploring the feelings of displacement and home.

Dr. Irwin Mark Jacobs

Irwin M. Jacobs has been described as "brilliant and creative," "incredibly innovative and undaunted," "business savvy," and "ethical." He is an industry leader, a forward thinker, a problem solver, a generous philanthropist, and a loving husband and father. When Dr. Jacobs packed up his family in 1966 and moved cross-country to accept a teaching position at the new University of California, San Diego, no one could have foreseen what his decision would mean to the future of La Jolla and San Diego. At UCSD he worked as a professor of computer science and engineering, then became an entrepreneur, cofounding Linkabit Corporation and later Qualcomm Incorporated, a giant in the field of digital wireless communications. U.S. President Bill Clinton awarded him with the National Medal of Technology and Innovation. Dr. Jacobs and his wife, Joan, have served on committees, councils, and boards, sharing of their time and wealth with educational institutions, arts associations, public television, and museums. When they came to UCSD in the 1960s, they probably never imagined that the university's engineering departments would one day become The Irwin & Joan Jacobs School of Engineering.

Black's Beach

William H. Black owned the La Jolla Farms horse stable and real estate development above the beach that was named for him in the 1940s. Black's Beach lies between La Jolla Shores and Torrey Pines State Beach. The northern part of Black's is a swimsuit-optional beach owned and managed by the State of California. Access is a challenge. The hiking trail from the Torrey Pines Gliderport is steep and can be dangerous due to the eroding and unstable sandstone cliffs.

The Mushroom House

Dolphins and surfers riding the waves off the south end of Black's Beach have a sea-level view of the Bell Pavilion, better known as the "Mushroom House." Designed by California architect Dale Naegle in the mid-1960s, the isolated guest house was built to withstand high waves, earthquakes, and rock slides. Connecting the Pavilion's building site to then-owner Sam Bell's main house 300 feet above was a challenge taken on by Elevator Electric Inc., which in 1956 built the nation's first exterior glass elevator—the Starlight Express—in the El Cortez Hotel overlooking downtown San Diego. The Pavilion's funicular-style tramway treats riders to spectacular views of La Jolla Shores and the Pacific Ocean.

Torrey Pines Gliderport

The westerly onshore sea breeze hits the 300-foot-high cliffs of Torrey Pines and creates lift. Since the late 1920s sailplane pilots have been taking advantage of this phenomenon in La Jolla just as the birds do. Aviators launch from the Torrey Pines Gliderport and ride the winds, soaring along the cliffs' edge. Pilots had to take a break during World War II when Camp Callan occupied the mesa, but afterwards gliding took off with the addition of radio-controlled model airplanes, hang gliders, and paragliders, all of them working with nature, not against it. A variety of new aviation technologies were tested at the gliderport, and the site has been designated a San Diego Historical Landmark.

Salk Institute

Jonas Salk, a scientist physician, developed the first safe and effective polio vaccine in the early 1950s while working at the University of Pittsburgh. With a dream of creating a research center of international scientists collaborating in a search for cures, he came to La Jolla and founded the Salk Institute for Biological Studies. Architect Louis Kahn designed the concrete, mirror-image laboratory buildings and central plaza. The institute's architecture showcases the ocean view and is just steps away from UCSD and the Torrey Pines Gliderport.

Torrey Pines Golf Course

Torrey Pines is a championship golf course with two 18-hole courses that
are owned and operated by the City of San Diego. Its coastal views, sheer
sandstone cliffs, rugged canyons, and rare Torrey pine trees distinguish it as
one of the most scenic golf courses in the world. Before the land was set aside
in 1956 to be made into a public golf course, it was used during World War II
by Camp Callan, a U.S. Army training center for anti-aircraft and coastal
artillery. Today golfers battle each other in friendly competitions. The most
memorable battle took place during the 2008 U.S. Open. Tiger Woods, limping
on his injured left leg, beat Rocco Mediate in a sudden-death playoff.

Farmers Insurance Open

The annual Farmers Insurance Open, a PGA Tour event held at Torrey Pines Golf Course each winter, brings worldwide attention to La Jolla. The best golfers compete on two courses, the North and the South. Phil Mickelson, Tiger Woods, Jason Day, and Bubba Watson are a few of the past champions of what began here in 1968 as the Andy Williams San Diego Open.

The Lodge at Torrey Pines

Owned and operated by the Evans family, The Lodge at Torrey Pines invites guests to get away from the hustle and bustle of daily life. The luxury hotel, designed in the tradition of the early 1900s' California Craftsman style, includes a spa and is at the edge of the championship Torrey Pines Golf Course. Also nearby are the hiking trails of Torrey Pines State Natural Reserve.

Torrey Pines State Natural Reserve

Torrey Pines State Natural Reserve began as a public park in 1899. Philanthropist Ellen Browning Scripps expanded the park by purchasing adjoining property and donating it to the people of San Diego. The Torrey pine, *Pinus torreyana*, a rare tree found in the wild here and on Santa Rosa Island, was named for botanist John Torrey. Scripps and others sought to protect the trees and park from damage and development. However, as the park continued to expand it needed more protection than the City of San Diego could provide. In 1956 a special election allowed the park to become a state reserve. There are strict rules for everyone to follow, such as no dogs or drones anywhere, and no food or drink other than water in the reserve above the beach. The hiking trails and beach are popular destinations for locals and visitors.

Torrey Pines Lodge Visitor Center and Museum Shop

Early visitors driving Ford Model T automobiles up the park's steep incline often stopped at the Torrey Pines Lodge, a restaurant. Ellen Browning Scripps commissioned the construction of the adobe-block lodge that was completed in 1923. Today it is the home of the Reserve's Visitor Center, Museum Shop, and Ranger Station.

Torrey Pines State Beach

Willets, sanderlings, and long-billed curlews are just a few of the shorebirds that feed and skitter along the wet sands of Torrey Pines State Beach. This wild, unspoiled stretch of beach, part of the Torrey Pines State Natural Reserve, runs for 4½ miles beginning at Black's Beach and ending in the southern part of Del Mar. The sandstone cliffs are continually eroding so it is best to keep a safe distance from their base. Strong ocean currents can create dangerous swimming conditions here. Staying in sight of the lifeguard towers at the north end is recommended. Low tide is a great time for jogging and strolling along Torrey Pines State Beach.

Torrey Pines State Beach on a foggy morning.

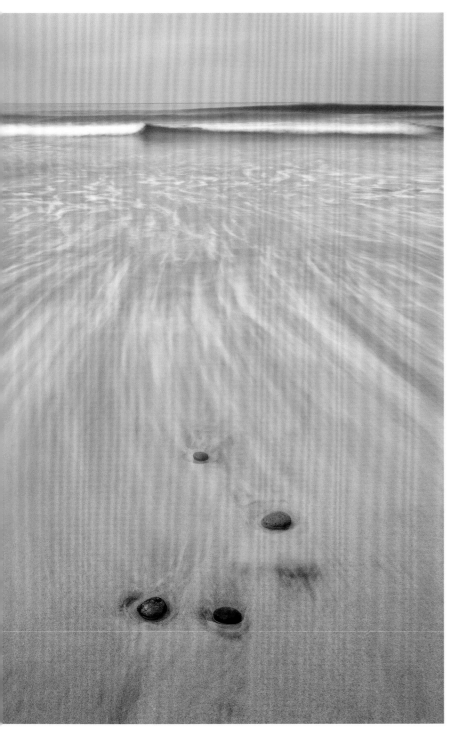
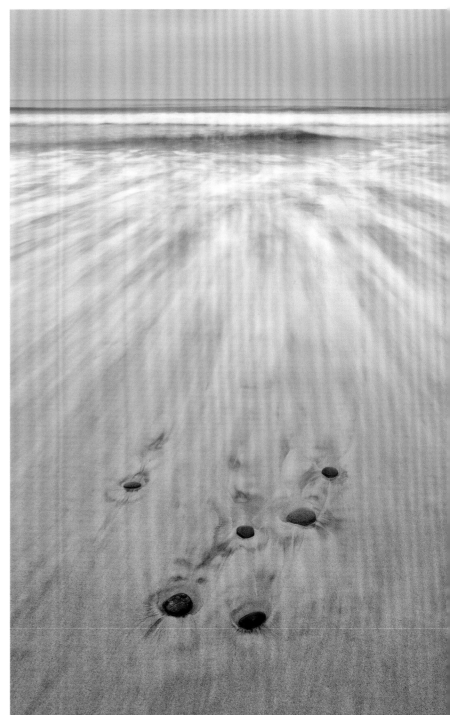

The Cross

On a clear day visitors to the top of Mount Soledad can see as far as Mexico to the south and Catalina Island to the northwest. Since 1954 the current cross, 43-feet tall from its fenced-in base, has towered above the mountain. However, La Jollans nearly lost it due to lawsuits filed regarding the Christian symbol's presence on government-owned land. After 25 years of controversy the land was sold to the Mt. Soledad Memorial Association, ensuring that the cross would remain. Today the memorial has grown to include U.S. Veterans living and deceased. Branches of service include the U.S. Army, Navy, Marines, Air Force, Coast Guard, and WWII Merchant Marine. The Mt. Soledad National Veterans Memorial encompasses walls of black granite plaques that share photos and stories of individual veterans.

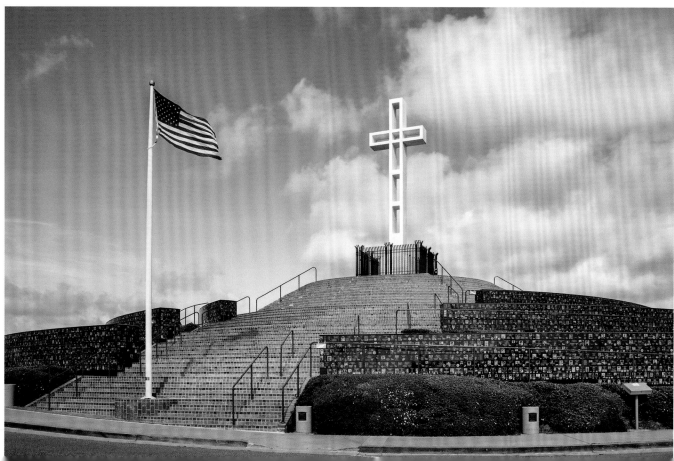

Christmas Parade

Despite a lack of snow and freezing temperatures in La Jolla, there is no shortage of holiday cheer. In early December residents line the sidewalks of Girard Avenue and Prospect Street to enjoy the La Jolla Christmas Parade & Holiday Festival. Floats, marching bands, riders on horseback, surf clubs, dancers, adopt-a-dog groups, and dignitaries riding in vintage automobiles traverse the parade route, all of them forerunners to the arrival of the guest of honor—Santa Claus.

Sunset from Marine Street Beach.

La Jolla Country Club

Coast Walk

Goldfish Point

The Cave Store

Silverado St

Ivanhoe Ave

San Diego-La Jolla Underwater Park

Cave St

La Jolla Elementary School/ Open Aire Market

Brockton Villa

Congregational Church of La Jolla

Harry's Coffee Shop

La Jolla Cove

Post Office

Herschel Ave

Point La Jolla

Prospect St

Silverado St

Mary, Star of the Sea

Kline St

Scripps Park

La Valencia Hotel

Girard Ave

Girard Athenaeum Gourmet

Meanley's Hardware

Fay Ave

Pearl St

Center St

Boomer Beach

Wall St

Warwick's

Adelaide's Flowers

VILLAGE OF LA JOLLA

Eads Ave

Shell Beach

The Grande Colonial Hotel

Prospect St

Silver St

La Jolla Riford Library

Coast Blvd

St James by-the-Sea

Draper Ave

Jenner St

Wisteria Cottage

La Jolla Presbyterian

Coast Blvd S

La Jolla Rec Center

Children's Pool

Museum of Contemporary Art San Diego

The Bishop's School

Marine St

Wipeout Beach

Coast Blvd

Coast Blvd S

Coast Blvd S

Prospect St

Coast Blvd Park

La Jolla Tidepools

Whispering Sands Beach

Marine St Beach

EAST

NE

SE

NORTH

SOUTH

NW

SW

WEST